50 OF THE FINEST
Adult
Party Games

LAGOON
BOOKS

Series Editor: Heather Dickson
Editor and Games Compiler: Sylvia Goulding
Design: Rosamund Saunders
Illustrations: Lotty
Additional Contributors: Sheila Harding, Ann Marangos
Cover Design: Gary Inwood Studios

Published by:
LAGOON BOOKS
PO BOX 311, KT2 5QW, UK
www.lagoongames.com

ISBN: 1902813065

50 OF THE FINEST
Adult
Party Games

Introduction

We all know that it's not just children who enjoy playing games, so we've put together this book that includes 50 hilarious games for "grown-ups", which are guaranteed to put people in a party mood and get temperatures rising!

TYPES OF GAMES
At the front of the book you'll find ultimate ice-breakers, ideal games to play at the beginning of a party to help get people to mix and mingle. Favourites include *Cocktail Conundrums*, and *Cinderella and the Prince*. As you continue through the book, the games get progressively more rowdy and a bit raunchy! Make sure you invite a room full of beautiful people if you're going to play *Peepshow*.

HOW TO PLAY
Each game has easy-to-follow instructions, and explains whether you need to do any pre-party preparation and how to organize your guests through to deciding on a winner and what nasty forfeit should be paid out to the losers!

WHAT YOU NEED TO PLAY

If you need accessories such as a dice or a pack of cards to play any of the games, they are carefully listed. Generally speaking, all you need are a keen sense of fun and a willingness to throw conventionality to the wind and lay yourself open to public humiliation!

VARIATIONS ON THE GAME

There's often more than one way of playing a game so, wherever possible, we've suggested some "variations on the game". These could be far quieter or rowdier versions of the game, or ideas for adapting the game if you have more or fewer players. You have the option to play the game that suits the mood or your particular mix of guests.

FORFEITS

IN MANY GAMES, PLAYERS ARE FORCED TO PAY FORFEITS. NEVER AN EASY THING TO CARRY OUT, THEY ARE ALSO QUITE DIFFICULT TO MAKE UP "ON THE SPOT". TO HELP, WE'VE LISTED SOME SUITABLY SPITEFUL SUGGESTIONS WITH GAMES THAT CALL FOR THEIR USE!

WARNING!

Some of the games in this book involve drinking. If played with alcoholic beverages, we urge you to exercise moderation in consumption!

Have fun!

Contents

Adam and Eve

THE ULTIMATE ICE-BREAKER: A GREAT FUN PARTY GAME WHICH WILL ENSURE THAT EVERYONE MIXES AND MINGLES

HOW TO PLAY

Before your guests arrive, prepare sheets of paper with names of pairs that belong together, for example, Adam and Eve or salt and pepper.

As each guest arrives, pin a sheet on their back so that everyone else can see their name, but they are unaware of their own identity. Make sure you do not pin name pairs on guests that arrive together, or shortly after one another – this would make it far too easy. If you have invited an uneven number of guests, you could always have a triple set, for example, The Three Musketeers.

YOU WILL NEED:

ANY NUMBER OF PLAYERS

SHEETS OF PAPER WITH NAMES OF COUPLES OR THINGS

SAFETY PINS

?

Once all your guests have arrived and have their identity pinned to their back, ask them to find out who they are and, at the same time, locate their partner(s). To do this, each guest will have to mill around, read everyone else's

label, and ask them questions about themselves, for example, "Am I dead or alive?", "Am I a human being?".

WHO WINS

If a guest thinks they know who they are, they should approach their assumed partner and check with him or her if their guess was right. Every wrong guess counts as a point. Stop the game at any point, and impose penalties on those who have not guessed who or what they are, and also on those who have made more than three incorrect guesses. Everyone's identity should now be revealed. If you play a partner game next, people could stay paired up as they are.

MORE IDEAS FOR PAIRS

ANTONY & CLEOPATRA
LAUREL & HARDY
SIMON & GARFUNKEL
RONALD & NANCY REAGAN
EDWARD & MRS SIMPSON
MICKEY & MINNIE MOUSE
ROMEO & JULIET
LEFT & RIGHT
YES & NO

VARIATIONS ON THE GAME

Last Names. Use first and last name pairs, as in Sadam & Hussein, Bill & Clinton. Add to the confusion, by having some last names with two possible first names: Jimmy, Donny and Mary Osmond, or Rupert and Iris Murdoch.

Cocktail Conundrums

THIS IS A GOOD TEST TO SEE HOW
CONVERSATIONS BETWEEN STRANGERS – AND
FRIENDS – DEVELOP!

HOW TO PLAY

Before the party, write a number of
phrases or statements on pieces of
paper. You could have a lot of fun
preparing this in advance!

Make the sentences as strange
or as silly as you like, for example,
"some people still believe the Moon
is made from cheese", "goldfish have
a short memory", "your flies are
undone", "there is more food in the bedroom", "the unique
selling point of paperclips", or "the government should call
for new elections". Fold the papers in two and place them
in a bowl or hat.

When your guests arrive, ask each one to pick a slip of
paper with a statement on it. Then explain that they need
to try to slip their phrase into the conversation, without
anyone noticing. This is not as easy as it may sound …

just imagine slipping a banal phrase like "there's some more food in the bedroom upstairs" into a heated discussion about world politics!

WHO WINS

As soon as a listener suspects that "a phrase" has been used in conversation, they need to challenge the speaker. If they were right, they collect a point. If they were wrong, they lose one.

Meanwhile, each time the speaker manages to plant their phrase without the listeners noticing, they collect a point, too. They will have to reveal to the listener once this has happened, to have their point verified. You could, of course, try to plant the same phrase more than once with the same speaker…

VARIATION ON THE GAME

FOREIGN PHRASES. Give each guest a phrase in a foreign language. This will be even more difficult to "plant" without anyone noticing if people add their own foreign expressions to confuse their listeners, such as "déjà vu", "o mama mia", "gesundheit" or "je ne sais quoi".

Cinderella and the Prince

THIS IS ANOTHER GREAT ICE-BREAKER WHICH
WILL GET COMPLETE STRANGERS TALKING
TOGETHER AS IF THEY WERE LIFE-LONG FRIENDS

HOW TO PLAY

This is a very simple game which
demands absolutely no preparation.
As guests arrive, ask them to take
their shoes off. Place all shoes neatly
along one side in the hall. Not everyone
will be happy with this — especially if they are
wearing holey socks! — but all objections should be
discouraged and worries assuaged. Just point out how
liberating it is to walk around barefoot!

    Now get each guest to take a shoe that is not theirs.
Their task is to find Cinderella, the owner of the shoe. This
game demands, of course, that everyone cooperates. If a
player walks into the room with a shoe, and the owner
instantly exclaims "That's mine!", it will be over very quickly.

    Instead, guests should scrutinize each other, try to
judge shoe sizes and styles, and eventually, when they

YOU WILL NEED:
TEN OR MORE PLAYERS,
WHO POSSIBLY DON'T
ALL KNOW EACH
OTHER

?

think they may have found a potential wearer, they should ask the person to kindly try on the shoe.

Imagine the fun asking the best-looking man in the room to try on a bright red stiletto, or getting a fashion-conscious young woman to slip into a pair of trainers. It won't take you any closer to becoming the winner but it's guaranteed to spark some interesting conversation!

WHO WINS

Each time a guest picks the wrong person to try on their shoe, they are awarded a pumpkin point. At the end of the game, the person with the fewest pumpkin points is the Prince. Those with the most points could be given forfeits.

VARIATION ON THE GAME

If you are planning a sit-down meal at your party, guests should sit next to the person with whom their shoes matched. The head of the table should be reserved for the "Prince".

FORFEITS

1. NAME 5 GRIMM'S FAIRY TALES

2. MAKE YOUR WAY ACROSS THE ROOM TO THE DRINKS CUPBOARD, ONCE YOU'VE BEEN BLINDFOLDED AND SPUN AROUND THREE TIMES.

3. SWAP SHOES WITH SOMEONE OF THE OPPOSITE GENDER AND WALK AROUND IN THESE FOR THE REST OF THE EVENING.

!

Alter Ego

ROLE-PLAYING CAN BE LIBERATING. BE WARNED,
EVEN SHY WALLFLOWERS MAY TURN INTO
PARTY ANIMALS!

HOW TO PLAY

Some time before the party, prepare your invitations.
Assign each invitee a particular character,
and ask them to act the part for all, or
most, of the evening. They could be,
for example, Pamela Anderson or
someone from the South Park
cartoons. Prepare your role
assignments at least a couple of weeks
before the party, so that your friends will have time
to sort out any suitable clothing (if they wish) or to swot
up on the character they are supposed to play. It all adds
to the fun.

**YOU WILL
NEED:**
INVITATIONS TO SEND
OUT BEFORE THE PARTY
ANY NUMBER OF
GUESTS

?

   At the party, everyone will (hopefully) act the part they
have been given – and all other guests should try to guess
who they are. You could carry on all evening, or call it a day
after an hour or so. Some people have been known to take
to this game so much, they carried on in their adopted
persona for weeks!

WHO WINS

Every correct guess of someone's role merits 2 points — one for the guesser, one for the role-player, for it is a sure sign of thespian talent if you can represent a character so well it is immediately recognized! Those who still remain *incognito* at the end of the game should be asked to perform a forfeit — one that doesn't involve acting!

IDEAS FOR ROLES

NANCY REAGAN

JOHN LENNON

TOM SAWYER

QUEEN ELIZABETH II

ROBERT DE NIRO

IDI AMIN

MADONNA

MARIE ANTOINETTE

J R EWING

VARIATIONS ON THE GAME

ALL PLAY TOGETHER. Instead of giving people unrelated roles and characters to play, make them all part of one drama or TV series. This should be well-known — Hamlet or Friends, for example — and will enable everyone to interact with everyone else.

IDENTICAL TWINS. Another great ruse would be to assign some (or all) characters twice — see if the identical twins recognize each other!

FORFEITS

1. MASSAGE THE NECK OF THE PERSON ON YOUR LEFT.

2. MASSAGE THE FEET OF THE PERSON ON YOUR RIGHT.

!

Hot Gossip

A GREAT GAME WHICH IS GUARANTEED TO STIR
UP SOME HOT GOSSIP ABOUT YOUR GUESTS...

HOW TO PLAY

YOU WILL NEED:
ANY NUMBER OF GUESTS
TRIVIA QUESTIONS,
PREPARED IN
ADVANCE
A PRIZE

Prepare one or two questions relating
to every person you have invited, for
example: "How old is Joanna's child?",
"What is Sue's mother's maiden
name?", "What colour is Dan's car?",
"What was Paul's first job?", "Where
did Chris go on his last holiday?", "Where was Debbie
born?", "What is Joseph's middle name?", and so on.

As guests arrive, they have to pick a question card, and,
during the course of the first hour or so, they will need to
find out the answer to the question. They can do this by
finding the person
mentioned on the card and
asking them directly, or by
by quizzing other guests
and eliciting all the hot
gossip from them.

There are advantages to both
approaches: guests do not have to

answer truthfully if asked direct questions about themselves. If asked about others, however, they need to give accurate answers each time – this, of course, makes finding the answers extremely difficult as – truthful or not – not everyone will know the personal details necessary to answer your questions.

Once you have found an answer to the question on your card, you can take a second card and have another go.

WHO WINS
This game engenders a great deal of chattering and gossiping – until the host or hostess calls a stop. The person with the most correct answers should win a prize for being "Top Gossip".

VARIATION ON THE GAME
RED-HOT GOSSIP. Compile only intimate questions such as "Who was the first person John slept with?", "What is the most unusual place where Paul has made love?", "What colour is Alison's underwear?", "When did Adrian lose his virginity?", "Does Mike close his eyes when making love?"...

Look-Out

THIS IS A PARTY "I-SPY" GAME WHERE STEALTH
AND CUNNING ARE THE KEYS TO VICTORY

HOW TO PLAY

Before the party, draw up a list of
objects in the house. These may
be unusual things, for example, an
ashtray from a famous restaurant
or a photograph of the family's dog,
which you have placed somewhere, but they may
also be part of your general household furnishings. Divide
the list into three sections: give 5 points for very obvious
objects, 10 for those that are more
difficult to find, and 20 for
those that only the truly
eagle-eyed will spy.
Make copies of these lists
and hand them and a pen to each
guest (or couple) as they arrive. Now
get the guests to try and locate all the
items on the list. As soon as they have spotted
something, they have to write down accurately on their
lists where the object is positioned/hidden. They have to do

this, though, without leading other guests to the hiding places, and without letting them copy anything.

WHO WINS

After a pre-set time, the host or hostess needs to collect all the lists and award points depending on the accuracy of the descriptions. The winner is the person (or couple) to have the most correct answers.

IDEAS FOR OBJECTS TO FIND

A PAINTING BY THE HOST

THE ENCYCLOPEDIA BRITANNICA

A BLUE TOOTHBRUSH

A BOTTLE OF BOURBON

A PEDAL BIN

AN AFRICAN VIOLET

A JAR OF BLACK PEPPERCORNS

A DRAWER FULL OF WOMEN'S UNDERWEAR

VARIATIONS ON THE GAME

Divide your guests into two teams, or if you have a bunch of garden enthusiasts among your friends, why not make this a specialist outdoor game? Everyone will have to spot and identify your plants – using the Latin names to make it extra difficult! You could, in fact, adapt the game to any specialist group. Get a group of art historians, to hunt for paintings, books and posters, or ask football fanatics to find different bits of football memorabilia and trivia strategically placed around the house.

Four-Letter Words

MAKE THEM MEET, MINGLE AND BE MERRY –
THIS GAME IS THE PERFECT WAY TO STOP PEOPLE
FROM STANDING AROUND IN CLIQUEY GROUPS

HOW TO PLAY

Before the party, prepare the sheets of paper, writing one
large letter on each one. To help you
choose letters, think of four-
letter words, including normal,
unusual and rude words, then
use all the letters in these
words (see ideas overleaf).

YOU WILL NEED:

AS MANY GUESTS AS POSSIBLE

LARGE SHEETS OF PAPER,
EACH WITH A LETTER,
PREPARED IN ADVANCE

SAFETY PINS

As your guests arrive,
randomly pin a letter on each one.
Ask them to find three others whose
letters, together with their own, will make up an
interesting four-letter word. Set a time limit, so you know
when to stop.

WHO WINS

When the time is up, get your guests to stand in groups of
four to present their word. Everybody else can judge the
result, and give points for originality. Unusual or rude

words get extra points. If one person — and their letter — features in several words, they also qualify for extra points. Points could also be deducted for boring and predictable words, or if two groups present the same four-letter word. The winner is ... the group with the most points, and they will have to organize the next game.

FORFEITS

1. NAME 5 FEMALE FILM STARS WITH BREAST IMPLANTS
2. NAME 3 OF ELIZABETH TAYLOR'S HUSBANDS
3. SPELL "PALAEONTOLOGIST"

If a group present their word in the wrong sequence (which is easily done, when you look down on your letter from above!) the whole group should have to pay a forfeit.

IDEAS FOR FOUR-LETTER WORDS

WORK / PLAY / LOVE / MINK / SINS / FOXY / QUIT
AND THE MORE OBVIOUS ONES ...

VARIATION ON THE GAME

You could assign different values to each letter. Difficult-to-use consonants such as X, Y, Z and Q score five points each, all other consonants count as two points, and all vowels as one point. The team with the most points wins.

Scrutiny

THIS GAME WILL PROVIDE YOUR GUESTS WITH THE CHANCE TO SCRUTINIZE EACH OTHER VERY, VERY CLOSELY!

HOW TO PLAY

Have a number of small objects ready to give to each guest as they arrive. Plastic toys are a particular favourite, but see below for more ideas. Guests should now hide this object on their person, so that it shows just ever so slightly. They could be tucked into trouser turn-ups, for example, hidden under the collar, or in a pocket, poking out of a sock or a belt buckle, nestling in the hair or tightly clamped in the armpit. Players should try to aim for a very slight, tantalizing, occasional glimpse.

The evening now progresses in its normal way, with everyone mingling, talking to each other, drinking and eating, or whatever else lies in store.

YOU WILL NEED:

ANY NUMBER OF PLAYERS

SMALL OBJECTS, SAME NUMBER AS PLAYERS

?

Towards the end of the party, or at any other point in time, the host or hostess should ask everyone to sit down and list all the objects they have spotted during the evening.

This, obviously, becomes even more difficult if your guests carry small objects on their body anyway – for example hair clips, bracelets, earings or handkerchiefs. To mislead others, players could tuck away apparel such as scarves, hairbands or belts – half hidden, half obvious to scrutiny – to make it look as if these are some of the objects designed to be spotted.

IDEAS FOR OBJECTS

PIPE CLEANER
FEATHER
PLASTIC FARMYARD ANIMAL
SAFETY PIN
SET OF CAR KEYS
PLAYING CARD
AN OLD PHOTOGRAPH
RUBBER BAND
ENVELOPE
A COUPLE OF DICE
RULER

WHO WINS

The full list of hidden objects is read out, and every correct identification earns the scrutineer a point, while every wrongly identified object loses a point. The player with the most points, wins. He or she should be given a prize – and then they should organize the next game!

All Change

THIS MAY SOUND LIKE A "LATE-NIGHT" PARTY
GAME, BUT, IN FACT, IT'S A GREAT GAME TO GET
A PARTY GOING

HOW TO PLAY

**YOU WILL
NEED:**
ANY NUMBER OF
MERRY GUESTS
?

Set aside two rooms or screened-off
areas as changing rooms, one for
women, one for men. On arrival, get
two people at a time to go to the
changing rooms and swap their clothes.
That's all there is to it – it's
one of the simplest things to do, yet the
effect is going to be quite
dramatic. Not only will some
people look strange, even
ridiculous, in another person's
outfit, but they will feel strangely liberated,
as they don't have to be their usual selves.
They can feel free to do or say almost
anything!

Some guests may have spent hours preparing
themselves and their party wear for the occasion – you
might need all your powers of persuasion to get them to

swap their fabulous designer gear for someone else's scruffy jeans and T-shirt, but it'll be worth the effort when you see how everyone behaves in one another's clothes.

VARIATIONS ON THE GAME

You could of course play this game at any time during the evening, but guests may feel more easily prepared to let go of their clothes – and their identities – after a few drinks.

If you opt for this approach, prepare small bits of paper with everyone's name on, place all the women's names in one bowl, all the men's in another. Now make everyone pick their costume of the evening from the opposite gender. Leaving the match to chance produces some hilarious results.

If your guests are sufficiently inebriated, or in a generally rowdy, saucy and flirtatious mood, you might find that you'll need only one changing room for everyone to swap their clothes in...

Pooled Resources

MOST PEOPLE THINK THEY'RE TEAM PLAYERS – HERE'S THEIR CHANCE TO PROVE IT!

HOW TO PLAY

If you are one of those people who carry around vast mountains of incredibly "useful" rubbish with you, whether in your handbag or in your trouser pockets, then this could be the game for you!

YOU WILL NEED:

A LARGE GROUP OF GUESTS
SEVERAL COPIES OF A LIST, PREPARED IN ADVANCE

The idea of "Pooled Resources" is for people to work together as a team to find the items on a carefully prepared list of "objects". Before the party begins, prepare the list of required objects, and make sure that the items are likely to be found among your guests. No one is seriously likely to have a cuddly bear or a toaster tucked away anywhere, so keep to everyday items like a pencil, a lipstick and a postage stamp. Remember also to have sufficient spare copies of your list for all guests.

Divide everyone into smaller groups of about five or six people, depending on the overall number of guests. For best results, make a list of all those you have invited, and decide in advance who you want to team up with whom for this game.

Give the starting signal and provide each team with a list. They now have to pool their resources, and find the required items among themselves. If no one in the team admits to carrying a particular item, the team has to beg, steal, or borrow from other teams, possibly swapping their own surplus items that others might need for the missing objects on their own list.

IDEAS FOR ITEMS

USED BUS TICKET
CONDOM
SAFETY PIN
CREDIT CARD
VIAGRA PILLS
CHEWED PENCIL
AN ASPIRIN
PHOTO OF PET (OR LOVER)
USED PAPER TISSUE

WHO WINS

The winning team is the first one to have found all the required items.

Think and Drink

THIS CARD-AND-WORD DRINKING GAME IS A
GREAT ONE TO GET YOUR GUESTS INTO THE
PARTY MOOD

HOW TO PLAY

YOU WILL NEED:
A PACK OF CARDS
A SMALL GLASS OF BEER OR
WINE FOR EACH PLAYER
FOUR OR MORE PLAYERS

Take a pack of cards, and remove all cards with a value from 2 to 7 inclusive. Place a full beer or wine glass for each player in the middle of the table, then arrange the remaining cards in a circle around the glasses, face down.

Now the first player turns over a card from the circle. Its value will determine what they will have to do:

Ace – no action for the first three
    Aces, but all drinks to be finished
    when the fourth Ace is exposed
King – the player has to drink one
    glass of beer or wine
Queen – the player who has had
    the least to drink is given one
    glass to drink

27

Jack – everyone has to take a swig from their glass, without finishing their drink

10, 9 and 8 – the player has to think of a word association

WHO WINS

Once the first number has been turned over, the player says a word of their choice, such as "cloud". As soon as the next number is turned over, this player has to come up with a word association, for example "rain". If they hesitate, repeat a previously used association, or can't come up with anything, they'll have to finish all the drinks.

VARIATION ON THE GAME

DRINK AND STRIP. Turn the above rules into a more frivolous set, if you wish. An Ace could mean: snog the person opposite; a King: remove an item of their clothing; a Queen: remove an item of another person's clothing; a Jack: strip to your underwear; a 10: put one item back on; a 9: allow another person to put one item back on; an 8: strip to the waist, or any combination of these.

Animal, Vegetable, Mineral?

THIS IS A CLASSIC AND EVER-POPULAR GUESSING GAME

HOW TO PLAY

The object of the game is for players to find out who or what they are. Divide guests into two teams, A and B, and equip them with paper and pens. Each team now has five minutes to write down 20 numbered objects. When the time is up, play begins.

Team A starts by giving team B a number between 1 and 20. This determines the object on team B's list that team A will have to guess. Team A is allowed to find out whether the object in question is animal, vegetable or mineral – but no more. The egg timer should be set, and team A has to start questioning team B. Team A can ask as many questions as it wishes, but team B can only ever answer with "Yes" or "No".

As soon as team A has correctly guessed the object in question, members may choose a second number on team

B's list and continue guessing, until the time has run out.

Now it is team B's turn — whether or not team A has guessed its object. Team B chooses a number, and then has to guess the object of the same number on team A's list.

FORFEITS

1. ANSWER "YES" OR "NO" TO THREE QUESTIONS BEFORE YOU HEAR THEM: "ARE YOU STUPID? ARROGANT? RUDE?"

2. COLLECT IN 3 MINUTES: 1 MATCH, 1 BOOK, 1 SHEET OF TOILET PAPER, 1 BLADE OF GRASS.

3. NAME THE 12 SIGNS OF THE ZODIAC.

IDEAS FOR OBJECTS

A DOOR
A FINGERPRINT
A PYRAMID
A BLADE OF GRASS
A BLUE LAGOON
A HAMBURGER
A CD-ROM
A BULLET-PROOF VEST
THE EMPIRE STATE BUILDING
A PENGUIN
AN ONION
A SURFBOARD
A BARBIE DOLL
A SPERM
A HEARING AID
A SNOWMAN
A HURRICANE

WHO WINS

Each correct guess brings one point. The winner is the team with the highest number of points when play is halted. The losing team should nominate a player to pay a forfeit.

Art Gallery

AN ARTY VERSION OF CHARADES THAT WILL SHOW UP TALENT – OR THE LACK OF IT!

HOW TO PLAY

To play this game, the host or hostess should prepare a list of 10 objects or sayings in advance. Divide players into two teams, and get them to sit together at opposite ends of the room, or in separate rooms. The host or hostess (or another player as decided) needs to act the part of quizmaster and must go outside.

At the starting signal, one player from each team joins the quizmaster who will give them the first item or saying from the list of 10. The two players must then rush back to join their own teams, and start to draw the object. The other team members have to guess what is being drawn, but the artist is only allowed to say "Yes" or "No".

Once a team has guessed correctly, it sends the next player out, to be given the second object by the quizmaster. While the teams are guessing, they have to be reasonably quiet, so as not to give away any clues to the

other team. A word of warning: players with artistic temperaments may get very frustrated and start shouting, "It's obvious, come on, anyone would recognize it!", but this will bring instant minus points.

WHO WINS

The first team to have guessed all the items on the quizmaster's list, is the winner, but some vicious forfeits will have to be paid for any minus points.

IDEAS FOR OBJECTS
CUP AND SAUCER
PEANUTS
OYSTER AND PEARL
LOOSE CHANGE
DENTAL FLOSS
ATHLETE'S FOOT
A NIGHTMARE
A BRUISE
A LAPTOP DANCER

VARIATION ON THE GAME

ART DEGREE. Make the list of items progressively more difficult, starting with, say, an apple, then moving onto a bottle of tomato ketchup, and ending with abstract expressions or sayings, for example, bondage, nuclear fission or light at the end of the tunnel.

Kiss of Death

THIS IS ONE OF THE ALL-TIME CLASSIC PARTY GAMES, ENJOYED BY WOULD-BE SLEUTHS AND ACTORS ALIKE

HOW TO PLAY

Before the party, prepare one card that says "killer" and as many other cards as you will have guests, each with the word "victim". Once you are ready to play, each person should draw a card but keep their identity secret from the others.

Now the party can continue as normal, with people wandering around and chatting to each other – except that there is a killer on the loose!

The killer will – when they feel unobserved – establish eye contact with one of the other guests and blow them the kiss of death. This kiss kills within five seconds, and after silently counting to five,

the victim should therefore sink to their knees and die a horrible, noisy and extremely painful death.

WHO WINS

All victims have to try to stay alive while at the same time trying to deduce who the killer is. Once they think they have found them, they should loudly declare "I accuse Janet", or Lewis, or whoever they have identified — while of course trying to avoid the killer's gaze.

If a second player has come to the same conclusion, the accused must show their card. If it says "killer", the killer has lost the game. If not, game continues and the two accusers must arrange the next game.

VARIATIONS ON THE GAME

ZOMBIES. Once the victims have died, they will come to haunt the living. Each dead person will have their own method for killing off other guests, such as winking, bottom pinching or tickling.

Any killers feeling brave enough might like to attempt to kill their victims by physically kissing them rather than simply blowing them a kiss — this method might be much more dangerous, but it's also *much* more fun!

Poke 'n' Pop

A ROWDY GAME THAT WILL GET EVEN THE QUIETER GUESTS BEHAVING LIKE DEMENTED REJECTS FROM A TARENTINO FILM...

HOW TO PLAY

YOU WILL NEED:

A ROOM FREE OF BREAKABLE OBJECTS

AS MANY PLAYERS AS POSSIBLE

ONE BALLOON AND A LENGTH OF STRING PER PLAYER

Clear your room of anything (or anyone) fragile. Make sure your Ming vase is safely put away.

Give each guest a balloon and a length of string. Ask them to inflate their balloons (no, this is not the main challenge) and then tie it round one ankle, using the string.

When the start signal has been given, everyone has to try to pop the other guests' balloons using only one elbow. The other arm has to be held behind the back. Use of teeth or pins, or stamping on the balloons is strictly forbidden. Guests may have to get on their hands and knees in order to reach the balloons with their elbows.

Once your balloon has been popped, you are out, and should act as a referee, making sure no one uses hands, their arms or any forbidden tools to help them pop their fellow guests' balloons.

WHO WINS

To hold onto your balloon you may have to hop, skip and jump or crawl away from your attackers, possibly even fight a bitter duel. The winner is the last person who has their balloon intact and around their ankle.

VARIATIONS ON THE GAME

BLIND BALLOONS. Blindfold every player and give them a rolled up newspaper to pop the balloons with. This is an even rowdier version of the game as it will lead to indiscriminate bashing and poking.

BALLOON TEAMS. Divide your guests into two teams and give each team balloons of the same colour. Now you have to pop all the balloons in the opposite team's colour, being careful to avoid your own.

ALL AGAINST ONE. Players whose balloons have been popped, have to carry on popping others. This makes it much harder for the remaining players to survive.

String Along

THIS GAME IS GUARANTEED TO BRING GUESTS TOGETHER – BUT IT WILL ALSO TURN YOUR HOUSE UPSIDE DOWN!

HOW TO PLAY

Before the party, decide on how many teams you will form, depending on how many people you have invited to your party. Each team should have between four and ten members. Now get as many lengths of string as you will have teams. The lengths should all be the same, but a different colour. Cut up each length into 20–30 different sized lengths, then hide them all around the house.

Make sure you only hide them in places where you don't mind your guests searching – your underwear drawer may not be the best spot (see overleaf for some less intimate ideas)! It could also make sense to declare certain rooms out of bounds, for example your study.

At the party, divide everyone into teams and tell them their team colour. Give the starting signal and get each team to find as many lengths of their team's string as they can. Set a time limit, say 15 minutes.

WHO WINS

Once the set time is over, get the team members to tie their lengths of string together. Now measure all the lengths — the team with the longest string has won.

IDEAS FOR HIDING PLACES

UNDER A RUG OR THE CARPET
IN A PLANT POT, HALF-BURIED
BEHIND CUSHIONS
IN A VASE
BETWEEN BOOKS ON THE SHELF
BEHIND THE CURTAINS
ON TOP OF A LAMPSHADE
TIED AROUND A DOOR HANDLE
IN A COOKIE JAR
IN THE MICROWAVE

VARIATION ON THE GAME

STRIP SEARCH. If guests come across another team's string, they should hide it on themselves.

Once the time is up, teams then have the chance to try and top up their finds by searching other team members. Caution: this could lead to a lot of groping and is best avoided if your guests don't like enjoying themselves!

Farmer Giles

THIS IS A FUN, BUT REALLY NOISY GAME.
YOU WILL SOON THINK YOU'RE LIVING ON A
LARGE FARM!

HOW TO PLAY

Before the party, assemble a number of small objects, for example, an apple, an umbrella, a postage stamp, a photo (see overleaf for ideas). Make several lists, with about ten small objects on each one. Add the name of a farm animal on each list, for example, pig, cow, sheep, goose.

Once your guests have arrived, divide them into a number of small teams. Each team should have about four to five people. Ask teams to elect a leader, and give a list to each team. Tell your guests if any rooms in the house are out of bounds.

Once the starting signal has been sounded, all team members need to try and find the objects on their list as fast as possible. Once they have found an object, they must not pick it up, however, as

only the team leader is allowed to do so. Instead, they should alert their leader by loudly making their assigned animal noise. The leader has to follow the noise and go to collect the find.

WHO WINS

The first team to collect all its hidden items, wins. All other teams should pay team forfeits.

VARIATION ON THE GAME

DOG KENNELS. In this game, everyone is a dog, so teams will have to be careful to bark in a distinctive way for their leader to recognize. Of course, you could always imitate another team's bark and thus mislead their leader ... Every time a leader follows the wrong bark, the team collects a minus point. The more points, the more arduous the forfeit!

FORFEITS

1. SING "AULD LANG SYNE"

2. CARRY THE PERSON ON YOUR RIGHT FOR 50 YARDS.

3. MAKE UP A LIMERICK ABOUT A DONKEY.

Clockwork Orange

A RELAY RACE THAT DEMANDS MAXIMUM COOPERATION – NOT TO MENTION SOME AGILITY

HOW TO PLAY

Divide your guests into two teams and line them up, if possible in a man–woman–man sequence. Now give the first person in each team an orange (or an apple or any other suitable object).

YOU WILL NEED:
TEN OR MORE PLAYERS
TWO ORANGES
?

As soon as the starting signal has been given, the first person places the orange between their knees, and turns around to the next player. The second player has to pick the orange up from between the first player's knees – but they will have to hold it under their chin. They are not allowed to use their hands.

Once the orange has been safely lodged between chin and chest, the third player will have to pick it up with their knees again. This is, of course, only possible if player No. 2 cooperates and bends down obligingly.

So the game continues, until the first team's orange has made it to the end of the line. If you have only a few

41

guests, you could prolong the race by going first down the line, then up again, back to the starting position.

WHO WINS

The first team to have raced their orange to the end of the line, is the winner. If the orange is dropped, points are accumulated which will result in a forfeit.

VARIATIONS ON THE GAME

KEEP-FIT. Add as many complications as you like. The third player could, for example, have to pick the orange up between their elbows, the fourth one with their teeth (without biting into it), the fifth between their ankles and so on.

PASS THE BUCK. Alternatively, you could use an old and crumpled bank note, and pass this from player to player between knees only. The less crisp the money, the better, as it will be more difficult to pick up.

FORFEITS
1. TAKE YOUR SHOES OFF AND JUMP OVER A CHAIR.
2. TAKE THE PERSON OPPOSITE AS A PARTNER AND WALTZ FOR 3 MINUTES.
3. TOUCH THE FOUR CORNERS OF THE ROOM WITHIN 15 SECONDS.

Wordsmiths

THIS CLASSIC GAME ALLOWS EVERYONE TO
CATCH THEIR BREATH – BEFORE THE NEXT
EXERTION. ALL YOU NEED TO PLAY IS A GOOD
IMAGINATION AND A WAY WITH WORDS

HOW TO PLAY

**YOU WILL
NEED:**
FOUR OR MORE PLAYERS
PAPER AND PENS
WORD DEFINITIONS,
PREPARED IN ADVANCE

?

Before the party, with the help of a
dictionary, prepare a set of cards
with definitions of unusual words,
for example, "leporine" (adjective,
like a rabbit or hare) or
"vermiculation" (noun, the condition of
being infested or eaten by worms).

When you are ready to play, the first player picks one of
the cards and reads out the word, and whether it's a noun,
adjective or verb, but they should not
reveal the definition. Now everyone
writes a mock-definition of their own,
trying to make it sound as
feasible as possible. Should
you happen to know the
meaning of the word, just
make up a definition anyway.

43

WHO WINS

The first player collects all the definitions and reads them out. Everyone now opts for one of these definitions as the true one, and writes down their choice.

The first player reveals the correct definition. Every correct guess brings a plus point, every wrong guess a minus point. The winner is the player who scores the highest number of total points at the end of the game, once all their minus points have been deducted from their plus points.

VARIATION ON THE GAME

MULTIPLE CHOICE. You could play this as two teams. Each team could have a set of words plus definitions. They could add two more definitions to each word, then pass everything to the other team. The other team would then have to pick the correct definition.

MORE IDEAS FOR WORDS

CORIACEOUS (ADJ) – LEATHERY

PARANYMPH (NOUN) – BRIDESMAID OR BEST MAN

NIDIFICATE (VERB) – MAKE A NEST

FLAVID (ADJ) – YELLOWING

FRUGIVOROUS (ADJ) – ONE WHO EATS FRUIT

CACHINNATION (NOUN) – PARTICULARLY HARSH AND PIERCING LAUGHTER

EDENTULOUS (ADJ) – HAVING LOST ALL ONE'S TEETH

OOLOGY (NOUN) – THE STUDY OF BIRDS' EGGS

Chinese Teapot

IN THIS VERSION OF CHINESE WHISPERS, YOU
PASS ON WHAT YOU *THINK* YOU KNOW –
WHICH MAY BE NOTHING LIKE THE ACTUAL
STARTING POINT!

HOW TO PLAY

**YOU WILL
NEED:**
TEN OR MORE PLAYERS

Ask all your guests to form two
teams, A and B. Everyone, except for
one person from each of the teams
(players A1 and B1), should be asked to
leave the room.

Player A1 thinks of an everyday activity, such as "frying
an egg" or "cleaning the windows", and acts it out to player
B1. B1 guesses what the activity might be, and asks player
A2 to come into the room. B1
tells A2 their assumption.

Now player B2 is called
in and player A2 acts out
the activity. Player B2
guesses, calls in player A3
and tells them. Player A3
acts out to player B3, and so on.

Basically, all members of team A know

– or think they know – what the activity is and act it out to members of team B, while all members of team B have to guess and pass their assumptions on to members of team A. You'll be amazed how quickly the activity changes from one person to the next, and with everyone in the room being "in the know", the newcomers will cause fresh rounds of laughter with each round of guessing and miming.

WHO WINS

There is no winner in this game – it is just fun to try and act well or "read" what has been acted-out.

VARIATION ON THE GAME

ADJECTIVES. Players have to think of, act out and guess an adjective, such as gorgeous, terrifying, clumsy. This is much more difficult, and the end result will almost certainly not bear the slightest relation to the starting point!

IDEAS FOR TEAPOTS
PRUNING ROSES
MAKING A CUP OF TEA
FLIRTING AT THE BAR
FINDING A TELEPHONE NUMBER IN A DIRECTORY
WRITING A LOVE LETTER
CLIMBING UP A SPIRAL STAIRCASE
DOING A CROSSWORD PUZZLE
HAVING A ROW WITH A NEIGHBOUR
COOKING SCRAMBLED EGGS

Bottoms

NOT A DRINKING GAME, BUT ONE THAT
BRINGS OUT THE NAUGHTY SCHOOLBOY OR –
GIRL IN EVERY GROWN MAN AND WOMAN!

HOW TO PLAY

YOU WILL NEED:
TWO OR MORE PLAYERS
PAPER AND PENS
A DICE

Players sit around a table, with a
large piece of paper in front of them.
If possible, use paper with a grid
that is large enough to write letters
into. Mark it out for yourself,
if you prefer.

The first player now
throws the dice, and thinks of a "rude" word with
the same number of letters as shown on the dice.
This word should be written into a central position
on the grid, either horizontally or vertically.

Now the second player throws the dice, and thinks of
another "rude" word which connects with the first word,
just like in the popular board game Scrabble™.

Players can challenge each other as to whether a word
is rude or not, and the person who came up with the word
will have to give a good explanation in what circumstances
or why this word could possibly be rude…

WHO WINS

A point is awarded for each letter. Previously written words that are lengthened by a new letter or letters, also count. If a player cannot add a word to the grid, they lose five points. The player with the highest number of points wins.

EXAMPLE

If player 1 throws a 6, they could write down "bottom" and earn 6 points. Player 2 throws a 5 and adds 5 letters to the existing one – for example a vertical "(b+) reast", also giving 6 points. Player 3 throws a 2, and turns the (s) into "sex", giving 3 points. Player 4 throws a 5 and writes "strips", which also lengthens "bottom" to "bottoms", scoring 13 points!

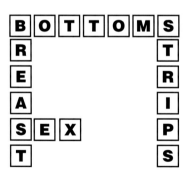

Sock Sumo

A SUMO-WRESTLING CONTEST – WITH A DIFFERENCE – IN WHICH EVERYONE CAN PARTICIPATE

HOW TO PLAY

YOU WILL NEED:

FOUR OR MORE PLAYERS

AN OLD SOCK (THE LONGER THE BETTER)

TWO LARGE NAPPIES (OPTIONAL)

?

This contest is a knock-out game, so you could have several matches taking place simultaneously, and make the winners compete against each other in the next round. If you do this, you would of course need more socks. If you can bring your contestants to do it, add a touch of authenticity to the contest by making them wear large nappies over (or instead of!) their clothes.

Two contestants should squat down on their haunches, facing each other at arm's length. Both should take hold of the sock, firmly gripping opposite ends. When both players are

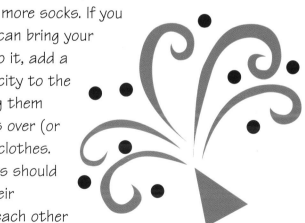

ready, the referee needs to shout "Go!", and the contest begins.

The object of the game is to get your opponent to lose balance and topple, touch the ground, or let go of the sock. You can do this by pulling the sock, but also by suddenly letting it go slack and "pushing" it forward while your opponent is pulling. Rapidly changing combinations of jerking, pulling and pushing are the recipe for victory.

When play is in action, neither player can touch the ground with anything other than the soles of their feet – which should not leave their starting positions.

WHO WINS

If either player touches the ground with hand, body or knee, or moves their feet, the contest is halted, and a point awarded to the opponent. The contest then re-starts. The opponent also gets a point, if a player lets go of the sock. The first player to five points is the winner.

VARIATION ON THE GAME

BLINDMAN'S SUMO. Blindfold both players for added difficulty. It is even harder to judge your opponent's intentions if you cannot see their face.

Haunted House

A SPOOKY GAME, WHERE GHOSTS HAUNT YOUR HOUSE...

HOW TO PLAY

YOU WILL NEED:

A MIXED GROUP OF TEN OR MORE PLAYERS

LARGE SHEETS FOR HALF OF THE PLAYERS

This game is best played by dividing your guests into teams of women against men, but you can of course choose any other grouping you please.

The men's team (or team A) should leave the room. The women's team (or team B) are the ghosts and stay in the room. Host or hostess will equip them with a large sheet per person. They should now adopt a position, on the couch, for example, with their legs pulled up, or leaning against a cupboard with one arm raised, and drape the sheets over themselves.

When the women are ready, the men's team comes back into the room. All the men have to try and recognize as many of the shapes as they can, telling each ghost their own name and who they think she is.

WHO WINS

Once everyone has made their guess, the female ghosts reveal their true identities, and award points for correct guesses. The winner is the man who recognized the largest number of ghosts.

Now reverse the game and send all the women out of the room, while the men become ghosts whose identities will have to be guessed by the women's team.

VARIATION ON THE GAME

TICKLE A GHOST. This should make it slightly easier to guess who's hidden under the sheets — and potentially a lot more fun! The guessing team is allowed to touch, feel and tickle the ghosts, making them squeak, squeal or laugh, so possibly giving their identity away.

You might need to appoint a moral arbitrator to make sure things don't get completely out of hand … unless your guests are happy for this to happen!

Aces High!

A QUICKIE GAME, THAT WILL GET EVERYONE ALL FLUSTERED AND OUT OF BREATH!

HOW TO PLAY

You will need the same number of playing cards as there are guests. If there are more than 52 guests, use two sets of playing cards. The cards should run in descending order, with the Ace counting high – so if you have 12 players, for example, pick out the Aces, Kings and Queens from each suit and discard all other cards. Spread all the cards out, face down, on a table in the centre of the room.

YOU WILL NEED:
EIGHT OR MORE PLAYERS
PLAYING CARDS
A TABLE
FOUR CHAIRS

All the guests should mill around the room, chatting and enjoying themselves. As soon as the host shouts "go", everyone has to grab a card. Those with an Ace are trumps. They should shout which suit they have, then quickly sit down on a chair. Now everyone with the same suit has to

join their trumps, and sit on his or her lap in descending order – the King of Hearts will sit on the Ace of Hearts' lap, the Queen of Hearts on his, the Jack on hers and so on, until everyone is "seated".

WHO WINS

The first suit to be correctly seated in descending order, wins. Every player who is found in the wrong suit, or in the wrong sequence of cards will have to pay a forfeit.

VARIATION ON THE GAME

SUMS UP. Decide on a total value of cards that ought to be seated together, say 25. Now players have to find the right combination of cards to make up the required value, no matter which suit they are, for example, the Queen of Hearts, the 9 of Clubs, the 2 of Spades, and the 4 of Diamonds. Assume that all faces count as 10 and all Aces as 13.

FORFEITS

1. CRAWL ACROSS THE ROOM ON ALL FOURS, BUT BACKWARDS.

2. CRAWL IN A ZIG-ZAG LINE BETWEEN EVERYONE ELSE'S LEGS.

3. CHOOSE ONE OF THE FOLLOWING STATEMENTS WITHOUT HEARING THEM FIRST: (1) PAY SOME MONEY TO EVERYONE IN THE ROOM NOW; (2) KISS EVERYONE ON THE MOUTH; (3) GIVE AN ITEM OF YOUR CLOTHING TO EVERYONE IN THE ROOM.

Hosepipe Ban

THIS WET TEAM RACE IS BEST PLAYED OUTDOORS, AND WITH ALL PLAYERS IN SWIMSUITS!

HOW TO PLAY

YOU WILL NEED:
TEN OR MORE PLAYERS
A TABLESPOON AND
CUP FOR EACH PLAYER
ONE BUCKET

?

Divide into two teams, or, if there are a large number of people, into several teams that will compete in a tournament against each other. Give a spoon to each player. Fill a bucket with water and place this at one end of the room or garden. Now place all the cups at the opposite end of the room or garden.

On the word "Go!", all players have to race to fill their cups with water, using only their spoons to carry the water from the bucket to their cups.

As everyone races simultaneously, mayhem is

guaranteed to ensue. Any player caught deliberately jostling another to make them spill their water, has to empty their next spoonful into their opponent's cup.

This game will be very chaotic, and most people will be soaking wet at the end of it. So it may be a good idea to ask your guests to take off their best party gear before they start ... You have been warned!

WHO WINS

The team to have filled all their cups with water first, are the champions — and should be doused with water, if they are not soaking wet already!

VARIATION ON THE GAME

SLOW RACE. You could make this race even more difficult — but also considerably slower — by getting each player to hold the spoons in their mouth as they try to carry the water across the garden to their cups!

Zip Boing Ding

A HILARIOUS QUICK-FIRE DRINKING GAME THAT'S EASY TO PLAY AND GREAT FUN TOO

HOW TO PLAY

YOU WILL NEED:
ANY NUMBER OF THIRSTY GUESTS
PLENTIFUL SUPPLIES OF DRINK

All players sit in a circle. One person starts, by looking at the person to their left and saying "zip". Player 2 immediately turns to the player on their left and also says "zip". Continue at great speed.

Now introduce the second rule: if you've just been "zipped", you can reverse the direction of play by saying "boing". Practise this for a couple of rounds, until everyone gets the hang of it. Of course it is perfectly permissible to "boing" someone who has just "boinged" you, making the play bounce like a table-tennis ball.

The third rule now comes into play. It allows any player to cut right across the circle by looking at any other player and saying

"ding". This player has to take up play without any hesitation, and decide whether they should continue playing to the left with a "zip" or to the right with a "boing" – or indeed a "ding"!

WHO WINS

Play at great speed, thereby causing more mistakes. Any mistake or hesitation is punished by a drinking forfeit.

VARIATION ON THE GAME

HANDSHAKES. Play the game to the same rules, but make players shake hands with the person to whom they are passing play. Merely introducing this extra action, especially if it involves getting up and crossing the room to shake someone's hand, will add to the error potential – and cause even more hilarity and drinking forfeits.

FORFEITS

1. FINISH THE DRINK ON YOUR LEFT.
2. SWAP YOUR DRINK WITH THAT OF THE PERSON ON YOUR RIGHT.
3. MIX THE DRINKS ON YOUR RIGHT WITH THOSE ON YOUR LEFT – THEN DRINK THE RESULTING COCKTAIL.

The Heat Is On

A SILENT DISPLAY OF ARDENT
PASSIONS – OR THE LACK THEREOF – TO KEEP
EVERYONE GUESSING

HOW TO PLAY

YOU WILL NEED:

FOUR OR MORE PLAYERS
TEMPERATURE CARDS,
PREPARED IN
ADVANCE

Before the party, prepare as many temperature cards as you will have guests. You can double cards if there is likely to be a large number of people. The cards describe the strength of attraction that one person feels for another, rising in degrees from "icy" to "red hot" (see overleaf for further temperatures).

At the party, choose two extrovert players who enjoy making a spectacle of themselves. Everyone else will make up the audience. Let these two actors pick a temperature card each. Now they have to act out their desire – without saying a word!

Observers have to try and guess the actors' feelings. The first person to have guessed one

temperature correctly, picks a card and joins in. Miming will become more complicated, because one person may feel "passionate" towards everyone else, and another will only have "lukewarm" feelings towards their fellow guests.

Curiously, this game becomes ever quieter the more people are acting, because the actors are, of course, not allowed to speak. You may, however, grant them the licence to laugh uncontrollably…

WHO WINS

The winner is … the first person to have guessed everyone's relationship correctly – this is very unlikely to happen, so you'd better just call the game off when everybody has enjoyed themselves sufficiently.

IDEAS FOR TEMPERATURES
ICY
STONE COLD
ALOOF
COOL
LUKEWARM
SIMMERING SLIGHTLY
WARMING UP
DEFINITELY ON HEAT
BUBBLING UP
BOILING OVER
VERY STEAMY
RED HOT

Dilemma

A VERY REVEALING GAME WHICH WILL REALLY TEST HOW WELL YOU KNOW YOUR FRIENDS

HOW TO PLAY

YOU WILL NEED:
FOUR TO TWENTY PLAYERS
PEN AND PAPER FOR EACH PLAYER

The aim of this game is to try and guess the preferences of another player. It tests your ability to read people's minds.

One player at a time is sent outside the room, while everyone else sits around the table with a sheet of paper. Players now think of a dilemma which they are going to pose to the player when they come back into the room. Thus, they could ask "Would you rather go around the world on a 50-ft luxury yacht or holiday for a year in the Caribbean?" or "Would you rather eat ten tons of chocolate or one frog's leg?" The better the

dilemma, the more fun the game. Thus you will really make your fellow guests sweat if you ask "Would you rather watch your parents in a porn movie or watch a porn movie with your parents?"

Before the player is invited back into the room, all others have to guess what their answer is likely to be and write this down. Now invite the person back in, and find out what their decision is – every correct guess brings a point. The game continues, with the next person leaving the room, and everyone else thinking up a new dilemma.

WHO WINS

The player with the highest number of correct guesses wins.

VARIATION ON THE GAME

Ask your guests to pair up and prepare "Would I rather" questions so that couples ask each other.

IDEAS FOR DILEMMAS

WIN THE LOTTERY OR WRITE AN AWARD-WINNING BOOK

SIT IN A TUB OF CUSTARD OR A BARREL OF WINE

KEEP A BANKNOTE YOU FIND IN THE STREET – TAKE IT TO THE POLICE STATION

STASH AWAY TOPLESS PICTURES OF YOUR BEST FRIEND OR SELL THEM TO THE PAPERS

MEET DAVID GINOLA OR NELSON MANDELA

Nose-to-Nose

THE IS A RELAY RACE, IN WHICH A LARGE NOSE IS A DEFINITE ADVANTAGE

HOW TO PLAY

YOU WILL NEED:

SIX PLAYERS (OR MORE, SEE BELOW)

TWO ONIONS

TWO MELONS

TWO CUCUMBERS

Mark out two lines, a start and a finish line, on the floor. Make sure the lines are not too far apart, as this game is quite difficult for the unfit. Divide guests into two teams, and appoint a neutral referee. The first players in both teams line up on their hands and knees at the start line, with an onion in front of each one. On the word "Go!", players push their onions forward, using only their noses. If any player touches the onion with anything other than their nose, they have to return to the start line. Once players have crossed the finish lines,

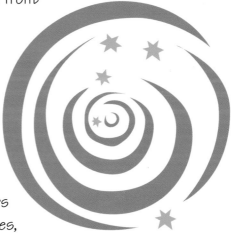

63

they have to turn around and return the onion to the start line.

As soon as the first player has crossed the start line again, the second player sets off, this time pushing a melon. Once they have returned, the last player has to manoeuvre a cucumber across the room and back. This is even more difficult, because oddly shaped cucumbers will not want to move in a straight line.

WHO WINS

The first team to have "nosed" all vegetables across finish and start lines, wins.

VARIATIONS ON THE GAME

MORE PLAYERS. If more than six players are in the race, add any number of other vegetables or other objects, for example two tomatoes, two cabbages, two peppers, two raw eggs…

NOSY TABLE TENNIS. Play this relay race using table tennis balls. They are very light, so will roll annoyingly, veering off into all sorts of unexpected directions, making the racer crawl after it in order to retrieve it.

A Pinch of Pain

THIS IS THE ALL-TIME FAVOURITE "MURDER IN THE DARK" WITH A PAINFUL TWIST TO IT

HOW TO PLAY

YOU WILL NEED:
TEN OR MORE PLAYERS
PLAYING CARDS

Select as many playing cards as there are guests, making sure that one of them is the Ace of Spades. Every guest draws a card. The Ace of Spades is the "Zombie Bottom Pincher", all the other cards are victims – people must not reveal their identities.

Turn the lights out. Now the Zombie goes around, trying to find a suitable bottom to pinch. Everyone else will be cowering in corners, trying to avoid the Zombie. As soon as the Zombie has found a victim and pinched their bottom, this person also becomes a Zombie, and the two of them now try to find other pinchable buttocks. If two Zombies pinch each other, they come alive again.

WHO WINS

There is no winner, and the game can be carried on for as long as people enjoy having their bottoms pinched!

65

Blowfish

A FISHY RELAY RACE WHICH REQUIRES
A BIT OF PUFF!

HOW TO PLAY

Cut out two identical fish, about
6in/15cm long, from newspaper.
Mark one in blue, the other in red,
on front and back. Mark start and
finish lines on the floor.

**YOU WILL
NEED:**
TEN OR MORE PLAYERS
TWO NEWSPAPERS
A BLUE PEN AND A RED
PEN
SCISSORS
?

Divide players into a blue and a red
team. Place the fish in front of the teams.
On the word "go", players get on their hands and
knees and blow to move their fish. There must be no
contact between person and fish. At the finish line, the
second player of each team takes over and blows the fish
back to the start. And so it continues, back and forth.

WHO WINS

The first team to have blown the fish back and forth
without cheating, wins – and is allowed to drink like a fish!

Go, Get 'em, Cowboys!

A WESTERN-STYLE MUSICAL CHAIRS TO TEST YOUR GUESTS' LIGHTNING REFLEXES – AND HOW THEY DIMINISH TO A DIM FLICKER TOWARDS THE END OF THE EVENING!

HOW TO PLAY

This game is best played by large crowds that mill around, chatting to each other, perhaps using several rooms of the house. The host starts it off, for he is Leroy, the fastest gun under the sun. Every guest – apart from Leroy himself – has to place a coin on a table or windowsill. Make sure this is in an easily reachable position, and far away from breakable objects, including glasses and bottles.

YOU WILL NEED:

ANY NUMBER OF PLAYERS, THE MORE THE MERRIER

A COIN FROM EACH PLAYER

?

The party takes its course, until – all of a sudden – Leroy shouts "Go, get 'em, cowboys!", upon which all guests dive towards the coins and grab one as fast as they can. Since Leroy himself knows when to grab a coin, one person will go without – and they will become the new Leroy.

Leroy should wait until everyone is well immersed in conversation again. Alternatively, it's also effective to

shout "Go, get 'em", almost immediately after you have just done so. Leroy is also allowed to mislead the cowboys.

WHO WINS

There is no real winner in this game, as the role of Leroy is continuously passed on to others. If, however, a false alarm has been given, for example if Leroy shouts "Go, get 'em, Indians!", all players who mistakenly grab a coin will have to perform a forfeit.

VARIATION ON THE GAME

COWBOYS AND COWGIRLS. Place one coin fewer than men are at the party on one table, and one coin fewer than women on another table. For this version you will need a Jolene to join Leroy. Both can shout either command "Go, get 'em, cowboys!" or "Go, get 'em, cowgirls!", at any time – which should cause no end of confusion!

FORFEITS

1. ANSWER THREE QUESTIONS WITH "YES" OR "NO" BEFORE YOU HEAR THEM: "DO YOU WEAR UNDERPANTS? DO YOU FEEL SEXY? IS THERE SOMEONE IN THE ROOM WITH WHOM YOU WOULD LIKE TO HAVE SEX?"

2. SHUFFLE ONCE AROUND THE TABLE ON YOUR BOTTOM.

3. KISS THE HANDS OF EVERYONE IN THE ROOM.

Hot Dogs

THIS IS A QUICK-FIRE WORD GAME WHICH REQUIRES PLAYERS TO BE SOBER ENOUGH TO COUNT THE LEGS OF A DOG!

HOW TO PLAY

Ask your guests to sit around a table or on the floor in a circle. The first player starts by saying "One dog, two eyes, four legs, goes woof on a roof in Duluth!". The next player then has to continue by adding another dog. So they will say "Two dogs, four eyes, eight legs, go woof woof on a roof in Duluth!". The third player increases the canine count and says "Three dogs, six eyes, twelve legs go woof woof woof…", and so on.

Anyone describing a mutant dog by, for example, saying "roof, roof" has to perform a forfeit and the

game starts again from scratch.

WHO WINS

The player that stays in the game without ever collecting a forfeit is the winner – and will have to down a large drink in one because they are obviously either a mathematical genius or much too sober to play such silly games.

VARIATION ON THE GAME

MULTIPLE DOGS. Instead of going around the circle, adding one dog per player, the speaker can pass play on to anyone else, and name the number of dogs. So "Two Dogs" could be followed by "Ten Dogs", for example. Make sure you set an upper limit, though. The party fun starts wearing a little thin if you have to sit all evening and listen to someone barking "woof, woof, woof … " one hundred times!

FORFEIT

1. GET UP WHENEVER SOMEONE ELSE GETS UP FOR THE REST OF THE EVENING.

2. TELL EVERYONE A DIFFERENT INTIMATE SECRET ABOUT YOURSELF.

3. SHOW ONE OF YOUR DISTINGUISHING MARKS (MOLES, BIRTHMARKS ETC.)

!

Figure Skating

THE WINTER OLYMPICS IN YOUR VERY OWN HOME – NO ICE, NO SKATES, BUT A LOT OF FUN

HOW TO PLAY

Appoint a Master of Ceremonies. Pair off all the players, preferably avoiding real-life couples, then give each pair a long stick of uncooked spaghetti. The first pair should go to the middle of the room, face each other, and put the opposite ends of the spaghetti into their mouths.

YOU WILL NEED:
EIGHT OR MORE PLAYERS
STICKS OF DRIED,
UNCOOKED SPAGHETTI
MUSIC

?

The Master of Ceremonies announces the couple and starts the music. The choice of music is important, as in real ice-skating. Classic waltzes or Ravel's "Bolero", as well as energetic songs like "Y.M.C.A." usually produce good results.

The couple now have to dance, displaying as much grace and enthusiasm as they can muster.

Standing-in-one-spot-and-bobbing-up-and-down is not allowed! The skaters will be judged on the ingenuity of their performance, so simple circling around will not bring very many points.

In addition to the judges' final verdict, the spaghetti stick poses a complication — once it has broken, the couple have to continue dancing, using the longer of the two bits only. This may soon lead to some very close dancing, indeed! (Watch out for those who deliberately break their spaghetti!)

Dance continues until the music finishes, or until a couple give up, possibly if they have got too close to each other for comfort. The second couple perform next.

WHO WINS

Everyone is a judge, and awards points out of ten to the other couples for Grace, Technique, Energy and — deliberate or otherwise — Closeness. The couple with the most points wins, and gets to choose the next game.

Matchmaker

HERE'S EVERY GUEST'S CHANCE TO RUB NOSES WITH THE OTHER PLAYERS!

HOW TO PLAY

Take a matchbox and discard all the matches and the insert, keeping just the outer case. All players sit around the table, or in a circle on the floor. If possible, try to get a seating arrangement in which men and women alternate.

> **YOU WILL NEED:**
> TEN OR MORE PLAYERS
> A MATCHBOX
>
> **?**

The first player has to place the matchbox case on his nose, and, once they've succeeded, pass it on to the player on their left, who will have to take it off them with their own nose.

This will involve considerable head-tilting, nostril-flaring and other peculiar movements and facial expressions. Absolutely no hands are allowed to help transfer the matchbox. For once, people with long thin noses will turn out to be the lucky ones – and they should never be called stuck up again!

WHO WINS

There is no winner as such in this game, unless you play it as a race between two teams. Anyone who is caught using their hands to help steady the matchbox case has to pay a forfeit, and anyone who drops the matchbox, has to pay a major forfeit.

VARIATION ON THE GAME

MATCH-A-NOSE. Play this game with two teams. Blindfold all the members of one team, and give half of them matchbox cases to pass on to the others. The other team has to direct and generally jolly the action along. There will be lots of laughter, as the blindfolded players are stumbling upon each other trying to pass boxes onto ears or other body parts!

FORFEITS
1. IMITATE A BABOON FOR 3 MINUTES.
2. ASK EVERYONE THEIR MIDDLE NAME, THEN WRITE THEM DOWN CORRECTLY.
3. TAKE OFF THREE ITEMS OF CLOTHING WITHOUT LEAVING THE ROOM.

Sardines

A HIDE-AND-SEEK GAME WITH A
DIFFERENCE – SUITABLE FOR FROLICS, BUT NOT
FOR CLAUSTROPHOBICS!

HOW TO PLAY

YOU WILL NEED:
TEN OR MORE PLAYERS

As in "Hide and Seek", one person goes off to hide, in a cupboard or behind a settee, or similar space. After five or ten minutes – as decided in advance – the next person gets up to look for the hidden player, but they have to do this on their own.

Once they have found this person, they have to squeeze themselves into the same hiding place. And thus the game continues.

As you can imagine, in no time at all you'll have the majority of your guests crammed into the tiniest cupboard in the house, jostling elbows in each others' faces, and trying to stifle any give-away giggles, while some lone soul is searching the house from top to bottom trying to locate the other guests.

75

WHO WINS

There is no winner, but there could be a loser – if the last person cannot find the rest of the party, the fun is over for them! You could also impose forfeits for anyone who gives the hide-out away by uncalled-for laughter or other noises. Some guests may, of course, try to provoke such noises by tickling or fondling their fellow sardines...

VARIATION ON THE GAME

LARGE HOUSES. If you have a large house, get everyone to search at the same time, but send them off in different directions. As soon as one person finds the hidden guest, they join them, being careful not to give their hide-out away to the others.

FORFEITS

1. IMITATE A VERY DRUNK PERSON AT THE POLICE STATION.

2. KISS THE LEFT EAR OF EVERYONE PLAYING.

3. COMPOSE A SONG ABOUT A GARDEN VEGETABLE.

Inquisition

A FAVOURITE PARTY GAME, THAT DEPENDS ON THE PLAYER'S ABILITY TO THINK BEFORE THEY SPEAK.

HOW TO PLAY

Choose a victim by tossing a coin. Now the player to the left of the victim starts by questioning them.

Questions should always start off "I saw you at the ... yesterday, and believe you ... . Is that so?" Thus the player could be told "I saw you at the nightclub yesterday, and believe you fancied one of the dancers. Is that so?" Some ideas for locations are overleaf.

As soon as the victim starts to answer, set the egg timer. The victim has to answer all the questions, but without ever saying "Yes, "No", "I", and without any hesitation. The questioner, meanwhile, will continue to bombard the victim with a whole barrage of questions as long as the egg timer runs. The questions will

always be designed to try and get a response which includes the banned words, and of course speed helps to confuse the hapless victim.

IDEAS FOR LOCATIONS
THE LOCAL JAIL
THE STRIP CLUB
THE BABY CLOTHES STORE
THE POLICE STATION
THE BUS DEPOT
A NUDIST COLONY

WHO WINS

Inevitably, the victim will fail, if sufficient pressure is exerted on them. Once they have said one of the banned words, they should be asked to perform some hideous forfeit. Should they last the course, however, they are released, and the role of victim passes to the next person.

FORFEITS
1. WHISTLE THE NATIONAL ANTHEM.
2. SING AND MIME AN ELVIS PRESTLEY NUMBER.
3. DO THE WASHING UP.

 ## VARIATION ON THE GAME

PONTIFICATION. Prepare some subjects in advance, the more spurious, the better. Now ask the victim to give a one-minute speech on this theme, again without using "Yes", "No", or "I", and without hesitating. Subjects could include the pollination of wild orchids or preparing supermodels for a fashion show. It's up to you!

78

The Last Straw

A SILLY RELAY RACE – GREAT FOR PEOPLE WHO WANT TO MAKE FOOLS OF THEMSELVES

HOW TO PLAY

YOU WILL NEED:
TEN OR MORE PLAYERS
TWO STRAWS
TWO BLINDFOLDS

Guests need to form two teams. Decide on an obstacle course through the room, for example, circling around the table, passing an armchair on the left, then a chair on the right, to return to the windowsill, the starting point.

Now blindfold the first person of each team, and give them each a straw. They have to clamp the straw under their nose, held in place only by their pursed lips. On the word "go!", they have to negotiate the course and bring the straw back to their team. There, the second person takes over the blindfold and straw, and negotiates the same course.

To make this race even more amusing to watch, the objects that had been outlined to the blindfolded person,

can be moved, either to a different position, or completely out of the way. There is nothing more hilarious than watching someone trying to negotiate what they think is a narrow passage, when they really have the entire room in which to manoeuvre!

In addition, you are allowed to distract the runner from the opposite team by giving misleading directions, shouting at them, or even tickling them. You'll soon discover that it is almost impossible to concentrate on the straw when so many things are happening all around you.

WHO WINS
The first team to complete the race and bring the straw back to its starting point, wins.

VARIATION ON THE GAME
CHEEKY COINS. This is a slightly ruder version, to be played at a later stage of the evening. There are no blindfolds or obstacles, but the players have to move a coin across the room, and drop it into a bowl. The coin, though, will have to be held firmly in place between their buttocks! Thus demanding great muscle control, and leading to some very amusing, slow shuffling. Hands are absolutely forbidden!

Take-over

THIS IS NOT A STOCKMARKET GAME, BUT YOU ARE MAKING A HOSTILE TAKE-OVER BID FOR THE OTHER TEAM!

HOW TO PLAY

Players form two groups, in opposite corners of the room. One person from each group now leaves the room, and outside these two decide together on an object. They re-enter the room, but will each join the opposite team – the player from team A will join team B, the player from team B will join team A.

The teams now fire questions at their visiting enemies to try and find out, as quickly as they can, the object in question. The player, however, is restricted to answering only with "Yes" or "No", but

they must be truthful.
Questions should be asked
very quietly, so that big-
eared opponents cannot
obtain any clues from the
other corner of the room
and use them for their own
purposes.

As soon as one team has found the correct
answer, they clap their hands and claim both
players as part of their team. Now each team sends
another player outside, and the game
continues in the same way.

WHO WINS

The winner is the team that
manages to take over all the
players from the other team.
This could take some time,
and fortunes may change, so
you might want to set a time
limit in advance and just count the
number of players in each team at that point.

IDEAS FOR OBJECTS
ROCKET LAUNCHER
BRA STRAPS
PORTABLE CD PLAYER
A BLADE OF GRASS
FULL MOON
SUMMER HOLIDAYS
BODY PIERCING
A ROYAL WEDDING

Touch & Feel

PLAY THIS GAME AT YOUR OWN PERIL –
YOU'LL SOON HAVE A WRITHING MASS OF
CONTORTED BODIES IN YOUR HOME!

YOU WILL NEED:

TEN OR MORE PLAYERS

SIX LARGE STICKERS PER PLAYER

PENS

A DICE

HOW TO PLAY

Ask each player to number their stickers from one to six and attach them to any part of their body or clothing. Where you put your stickers is entirely up to you – but it may make all the difference in the end!

Everyone should stand in a circle, and the first player starts by rolling the dice. If they throw a 2, for example, they have to place a hand or foot or any other part of their body on to one of the stickers marked 2 on any other player's body. They have, at this stage, a free choice of stickers.

Play continues, with the next player throwing the dice, and placing any part of their anatomy on the appropriately numbered sticker on any other player's body. Players must not lose touch with any

of the stickers they are already touching. Everyone is still allowed to move around the room as they wish – that is, if they are able to, because all their previous "attachments" will soon prove very restricting.

As players become more and more entangled, it will become increasingly difficult to remain in touch with their chosen stickers. Any player losing their balance, or breaking contact with their stickers, is out. Play continues without them.

If there is no free sticker available of the number rolled on the dice, play moves to the next person.

Players are allowed to "bump" and throw others off-balance – although this may, of course, make them stumble themselves.

If a player can no longer reach the dice, they must ask another person to roll it for them. The dice may be "rolled" with any part of the body, with the feet or elbows for example, but it must turn over at least once.

WHO WINS

No one! There is no winner, this game is just a great laugh to play ... and gives you the opportunity to feel up other guests – and be felt up yourself!

Zootime

A CRAZY DRINKING GAME WHICH WILL
TURN YOUR LIVING ROOM INTO A ZOO FULL
OF DRUNK SKUNKS AND PISSED NEWTS

HOW TO PLAY

Before the party, write the names of
animals – common or unusual – on
separate sheets of paper, and fold
them up (see overleaf). At the party,
each guest picks one animal card out of
the hat, and thinks of a noise and an action
to go with their new animal identity.

**YOU WILL
NEED:**
TEN OR MORE PLAYERS
ANIMAL CARDS,
PREPARED IN
ADVANCE

?

In the first round, each player in turn has to make their
animal noise and action. The other players have to try and
identify what they are – if nobody guesses correctly,
the player immediately has to pay a forfeit.

Once all players have "introduced" themselves,
the first player makes their noise and action,
looks at one of the other players whom they
wish to pass play on to, and makes that
person's noise and action. So, for example, they could
behave like an ape and make ape-like sounds, followed by
swinging their trunk and screaming like an elephant. The

85

next player, "the elephant", now has to follow quickly with their own noise and activity, before picking out a third player and imitating them. All this should happen at break-neck speed and without giggling. Of course you may mislead others by looking at one player and making the noises and actions of another!

WHO WINS

Laughter is to be paid with a minor forfeit, getting animal noises or actions wrong with a major one.

VARIATION ON THE GAME

BIRDWATCH. A simple variation in which all guests have to become birds. They should sing and fly around the room, landing with their hands on the shoulders of the next bird that they will have to imitate.

FORFEITS
1. DO A LAP-DANCE.
2. EAT 3 CREAM CRACKERS, THEN WHISTLE THE NATIONAL ANTHEM.
3. CONFESS YOUR WILDEST FANTASY TO EVERYONE PRESENT

Noise-You-Like

THIS IS A VERSION OF THE
CHILDREN'S FAVOURITE "SQUEAK, PIGGY,
SQUEAK" – DEFINITELY FOR THE SILLIER
PART OF THE EVENING!

HOW TO PLAY

YOU WILL NEED:
TEN OR MORE PLAYERS
ONE BLINDFOLD
A CUSHION
A TIMER

Like in the children's game, everyone sits around in a circle. One player is chosen to be in the middle of the circle. Blindfold this player and equip them with a cushion. Then either turn them around a few times until they become dizzy and thoroughly disorientated, or ask everyone in the circle to change places once the player is blindfolded.

Now the blindfolded player finds one of the other players in the circle and – without touching them all over, which might give their identity away – places the cushion on their lap and sits on it. They

now have thirty seconds to ask this player to make any noise of their choice. So they could ask for a pig's squeak, a tiger's growl, a buzzing bumble-bee, a hovering helicopter, a ship's horn ... the choice is entirely theirs. The sat-upon person has to make the noise they have been asked for, but they may, of course, disguise their voice.

WHO WINS

If the player cannot guess the sat-upon person's identity during an allocated time, they will have to move onto another lap. As soon as an identity has been established correctly, that person will be blindfolded.

VARIATION ON THE GAME

LAP DANCING. When the blindfolded player is seated on another person's lap, instead of asking for a noise, they can ask for a particular body part to be held out for them to touch, feel and guess. Again the person on whose lap they are sitting may conceal their indentity by presenting an arm when asked for a leg, or even substituting their neighbour's limbs ... A quick guess could be very revealing!

Peepshow

THIS IS A VERY OLD GAME, AND A VERY SILLY ONE, BUT IT STILL MANAGES TO SUCCESSFULLY AMUSE AND ENTERTAIN

HOW TO PLAY

YOU WILL NEED:
TEN OR MORE PLAYERS
A LARGE BLANKET
THUMB TACKS OR TAPE WITH WHICH TO ATTACH THE BLANKET
PAPER AND PENS

Suspend a large blanket over a doorway, leaving a small gap at the bottom. Make sure it is not see-through. If you are using a sheet instead, for example, the room inside should be well lit, so that no one can recognize shapes on the other side of it.

Players form two teams. If the company is mixed, it is a good idea to divide the teams according to gender. Not everyone will want to play, but try to persuade them – the more people who join in, the merrier the game.

One team leaves the room, the other stays inside. Those outside will have to take off their shoes, socks, tights, or roll up trouser legs, depending on which part of their body

is to be displayed through the gap left by the blanket screen. This could be the toes, but you can also decide to show feet, legs up to the knee, or, for the more athletic ones, ears, the inside of hands, or indeed any other parts of the anatomy if players are so inclined...

Players should walk up to the blanket and display, one by one (remembering in which sequence they showed themselves). Those inside the room confer and write down who they think was showing, in the correct order.

This becomes extra difficult, if some people know about the game in advance, for they could paint their toenails, shave off any tell-tale hairs, and disguise themselves in many other ways.

WHO WINS

Identities are revealed at the end, and teams are awarded one point for each correct guess.

VARIATION ON THE GAME

TOUCH & FEEL. Instead of showing a part of their bodies, all should remain concealed, but those inside the room are allowed to put their hands under the blanket and feel to guess the hidden person's identity! Could be ticklish...

All Strung Up

A GREAT GAME IF YOUR GUESTS ARE
INTO BONDAGE. AND IF THEY AREN'T,
THEY SOON WILL BE ...

HOW TO PLAY

YOU WILL NEED:
10 PLAYERS OR MORE
TWO KEYS
TWO BALLS OF STRING

?

Divide guests into two teams and line them up, if possible in a man–woman–man sequence. Now take two keys and two balls of string, and tie one key to the end of each ball of string. Hand the first person in each line the key, then give the starting signal.

The first player now drops the key through his shirt and feeds it out through one trouser leg. He passes the key to the next person, and she will have to feed the key up her skirt or trousers and out the top of her blouse, before passing it to the next player, who will pass it down his clothes again. All the while the key is still tied to the string, so that soon, all are tied up together.

Once the end of the line has been reached, the key will have to go back up the line again. If it came

91

out at the "bottom" of the last person, they will have to feed it through from the "top" next and pass it on, to avoid it becoming disentangled!

Guests will want to help each other get the key through as fast as they can, and grovel around in each other's clothes, because speed is of the essence.

WHO WINS

The first team to have passed the key all the way down and back up the line wins – and can start disentangling themselves, should they wish to!

VARIATION ON THE GAME

CLOSE-UP. String the key down the line only. Once it has reached the end, make everyone stand very close together. The last person holds on to the key, while the first person pulls on the string, hard enough to make the string as short as possible, but not so hard that it detaches itself from the key. Now cut the string, pull it out and measure. The team with the shortest string wins – which means that they will need to get REALLY close to each other. If you're going to play this version of "All Strung Up", make sure you pick the people you stand next to with care!

Male-Female?

A DRINKING BATTLE OF THE SEXES, TO SEE WHO'S GOT THE BIGGEST ... STAMINA!

HOW TO PLAY

YOU WILL NEED:
ONE PACK OF CARDS
ANY NUMBER OF
THIRSTY PLAYERS

Play this game when people are ready to laugh at themselves and have stopped taking themselves too seriously! Shuffle all the cards, and place them, face down, in the middle of the table.

One player picks a card. If it is a King, all the men have a drink; if it is a Queen, all the women have a drink; if it is a Jack, only the player who turned it over has a drink; if it is a 10, everyone has a drink. As simple as that!

If, however, an Ace is turned over, men and women have to change their clothes. After this, partygoers may no longer be sure whether they are male or female, and others might have justifiable doubts, too.

Therefore, if a 6 is picked, all men need to prove their gender – in a way that is acceptable to all the other guests, and if an 8 is picked, all women have to prove theirs!

Worst of all – if a 9 follows a 6, all guests have to strip completely!

WHO WINS

The winner is the player who can still walk in a straight line and knows whether they are male or female after all the cards have been turned over. Anyone who gets it wrong, though, and wants to take off their clothes when there is no need to do so, will have to pay a forfeit.

VARIATION ON THE GAME

For a rowdy, non-alcoholic version of this game, use the following code: Ace = men and women change clothes; King = all men whistle a tune; Queen = all women sing a song; Jack = everyone pays a forfeit.

Blind Date

A TOUCH AND FEEL GAME WHICH
WILL PROVIDE THE IDEAL OPPORTUNITY
FOR YOUR GUESTS TO GET TO KNOW EACH
OTHER, INTIMATELY

HOW TO PLAY

Play this game towards the end of the evening, once a few inhibitions have been shed, and when everyone has had a chance to get to know all the other guests.

Ask men and women to go into separate rooms. There they should pick someone from their group to be blindfolded. These two players will now be led back into the room, and seated on chairs that back onto each other.

On the word "Go!", both blindfolded players reach behind their backs to feel their fellow guest.

95

Fumbling continues, until the first person has made out who's sitting behind them. They are then awarded a point for the discovered identity.

The game now continues, with the next couple to be chosen by their teams as blindfolded victims.

As men and women select their victims in separate rooms, they do not know who will be paired up with them. This should help prevent deliberate and cruel mismatches of people who wouldn't normally wish to fondle each other. You could, of course, play this game with mixed teams – this will lead to two women – or two men – respectively fondling each other!

WHO WINS

The team with the most points, is the winner.

VARIATION ON THE GAME

THE BOTTOM LINE. Instead of seating the blindfolded couple back to back, they could be made to stand back to back, and made to rub their bottoms against each other. They will have to identify their partner by the feel of their buttocks alone...not easy, especially if they are wearing thick woollen skirts or leather trousers!

Ballroom Blitz!

YOU MAY HAVE PLAYED "STATUES" AS A CHILD. HERE'S THE ADULT, SLIGHTLY MORE RISQUÉ VERSION

HOW TO PLAY

One player is designated to be the DJ. If there is an even number of guests, you could have one DJ and one referee. All the other guests have to pair off. If there are more men than women, or the other way around, that's just tough — they'll have to pair up anyway as all-male or all-female dance partners.

YOU WILL NEED:
TEN OR MORE PLAYERS
BALLROOM-DANCE MUSIC
A TIMER
?

Now the DJ starts the dance music, and all the couples have to dance, beautifully, energetically and enthusiastically. In fact, they should aim to turn in a world-class performance if they can. All the classic ballroom dances are great for this game — waltz, foxtrot, rumba — but the tango has got to be one of the very best!

At any point, the DJ may decide to stop the music without prior warning, and all dancers have to freeze on the spot. This is why the tango is great — you may end up leaning backwards towards the floor, or in another equally absurd and challenging position.

All dancers have to maintain their position for five full minutes. The referee will keep their eagle eyes on the proceedings to make sure that nobody moves a muscle, twitches a limb, or worse, starts giggling! Should one of the players succumb, they will instantly be condemned to remove an item of clothing.

After five minutes, the music resumes, and couples are allowed to continue dancing — until it stops again. Play continues, until you have a room full of nude statues.

WHO WINS

The couple to keep their clothes on the longest, are the winners. However, since they are spoiling everyone else's fun, they should be asked to pay a hefty forfeit — both should have to strip to the waist and dance an honorary, semi-bare round to twist or rock'n'roll music!

Saucy Simon Says

THIS IS THE ADULT VERSION OF THE CHILD'S GAME – WHICH IS MUCH MORE FUN TO PLAY

HOW TO PLAY

All guests get in a circle around the designated "Simon", and hold hands. Simon now tells a story about himself, while all the players slowly move around in one direction.

YOU WILL NEED:

TEN OR MORE FULLY-DRESSED PLAYERS

Suddenly, and perhaps almost unnoticed because it is part of the story, Simon will call out a simple command, for example "Simon says, scratch your nose" or "Simon says, stand on one leg", and everyone immediately has to do as Simon commanded.

To fool all the players, Simon will pepper his story with misleading

commands that do not start with "Simon says". So, if Simon suddenly says "Mike says, clap your hands", or, without a name, "Hum a tune", players should NOT in fact clap their hands NOR hum a tune.

Anyone who follows the wrong command, or acts wrongly after a correct command, has to take off an item of clothing. And it'll be interesting to discover who makes deliberate mistakes, won't it?

WHO WINS

The winner is the last person to remain fully clothed – and they should be punished for being so subservient by having to fulfill one command from every person in the room ...

IDEAS FOR SIMON'S COMMANDS

KISS THE PERSON ON YOUR LEFT

TOUCH YOUR TOES

PINCH THE BOTTOM OF THE PERSON ON YOUR RIGHT

TURN ONCE ON THE SPOT, IN A CLOCKWISE DIRECTION

SWAP PLACES WITH THE PERSON OPPOSITE

TOUCH YOUR LEFT EAR WITH YOUR RIGHT HAND

WHISPER A TERM OF ENDEARMENT INTO THE EAR OF THE PERSON TO YOUR RIGHT

DO TWO PRESS-UPS

SLAP THE PERSON TO YOUR LEFT ON THE BOTTOM

Hide and Streak

THIS IS A VERSION OF THE TRADITIONAL
CHILDREN'S GAME – ONLY TO BE PLAYED BY
CONSENTING ADULTS!

HOW TO PLAY

**YOU WILL
NEED:**
FOUR OR MORE PLAYERS
HIDING PLACES
AROUND THE HOME
OR GARDEN

?

Just like in the children's game, one
player goes off and hides somewhere
in the house, and then everyone else
goes to look for them. Whoever finds
the hidden player first, becomes the
next person who has to hide and be
discovered by the others.

But here comes the "adult" element: the finder is allowed
to nominate one of the other players,
and this person will have to remove
an item of clothing. And so the
game continues.

Obviously there is a question
of attitude here. Players can be
either fair-minded, into equal
opportunities and generally
magnanimous – in which case they
will make sure that everyone undresses

at approximately the same pace. Or, they can be mean, wicked, selfish and unashamedly pleasure-seeking – in which case one poor soul may be singled out and victimized by everyone, and they will soon find themselves stark naked!

WHO WINS

There is no winner in this game. Or, to look at it another way, everyone is a winner of sorts – some people may prefer to keep their clothes on, but others may be only too keen to make a public exhibition of themselves and their state of undress!

VARIATION ON THE GAME

HIDE, STREAK AND SPLASH. In the summer, play this game out of doors for the best results. The first person to be completely naked, should be allowed to hose all the others down – this will be very enjoyable for those who like wet T-shirt contests, and it may also turn your garden into a nudist colony – for surely no one will want to keep on their soaking-wet clothes.

Balloon Shuffle

A LITTLE LIKE A THREE-LEGGED RACE, BUT IT MAKES WALKING EVEN MORE DIFFICULT!

HOW TO PLAY

YOU WILL NEED:
TEN OR MORE PLAYERS
TWO BALLOONS

Mark a start and finish line. Blow up two balloons, and half-fill each one with water, to make them more likely to burst! Divide guests into two teams, and ask people to form pairs.

On "Go!" the first two players of each team have to place and hold the balloon between their bottoms, then shuffle along to the finish line and back again, where the next two players take over. The trick is to press bottoms close enough together not to lose the balloon, but not so firmly that the balloon will burst – and shed its watery load over both players!

WHO WINS

When every couple in one team have taken the balloon to the finish line and back, they have won. The other team will have to either pay forfeits, or organize the next game.

103

Other titles published by Lagoon Books

GAMES BOOKS

50 of the Finest Drinking Games ISBN 1899712178
50 of the Finest After Dinner Games ISBN 1902813057

BOTTLE BOOKS

Lateral Thinking Puzzles ISBN 1899712208
Trivia Quiz ISBN 1899712216
Pub Joke Book ISBN 1899712224

All books can be ordered from bookshops by quoting the above ISBN numbers.

For more titles, visit the Lagoon Books' website at www.lagoongames.com